No one is going to hand your dreams to you. You must work for what you want. When you strive earnestly and consistently for a dream, you become the person capable of reaching it. The harder you work, the closer you get.

Grab firmly to your dreams and hold tight.

There is joy in giving your best to worthy pursuits. How you achieve your dream is how you live your life—intentionally, day by day. You can create what you want. Your dreams are counting on you. Your future is asking you to believe, to be brave, to make it happen. The most important part of realizing a dream will always be the dreamer.

What the day brings depends on what you bring to the day. Opportunity arrives with each moment.

When you open your heart to a dream,
love, hope, and excitement rush in.

Don't just discover your talents.
Make something incredible with them.

Choose your life. Don't settle for it.
You will regret what you didn't do
much more than what you did.

Spend your energy wisely.
Fill your time with things that fill your heart.
Breathe deeply into the possibilities of your life.

Do more of what sparks a fire in you.
Having something to strive for
brings its own kind of joy and energy.

Put work behind your good intentions.

Keep the promises you made to yourself.

It is important to attempt to do things you
are not yet able to do. Don't worry about being perfect.
Focus on growing, learning, and discovering.

When you strive to be better,
everything around you becomes better too.

Be willing to make mistakes, to mess up, to be disappointed.
Finding what's wrong can lead to discovering what's right.

Doubts can come from anywhere,
but the most harmful are the ones that come from you.

Fear can make things seem different than what they are.
Worry can give a small thing a big shadow.

Be brave. The quickest way to gain confidence
is to do the thing you are afraid to do.

Focus on what you can influence.
Make peace with what you cannot change.

Have the courage to admit when things aren't going
according to plan and the flexibility to adapt and change.

Good things can take time. Be proud of how far you've come,
even if it's not where you hoped you'd be.

Stay positive. It never rains forever.

Don't give up. The most important time to care and believe is when no one else does.

Pick up the pieces of your setbacks
and make something beautiful with them.

Don't wait until you've achieved
your goal to be proud of yourself.
Be proud every step along the way.

This is your life. This is your time.
Don't let it slip away unnoticed or unused.
Give your best to something
that is meaningful to you.

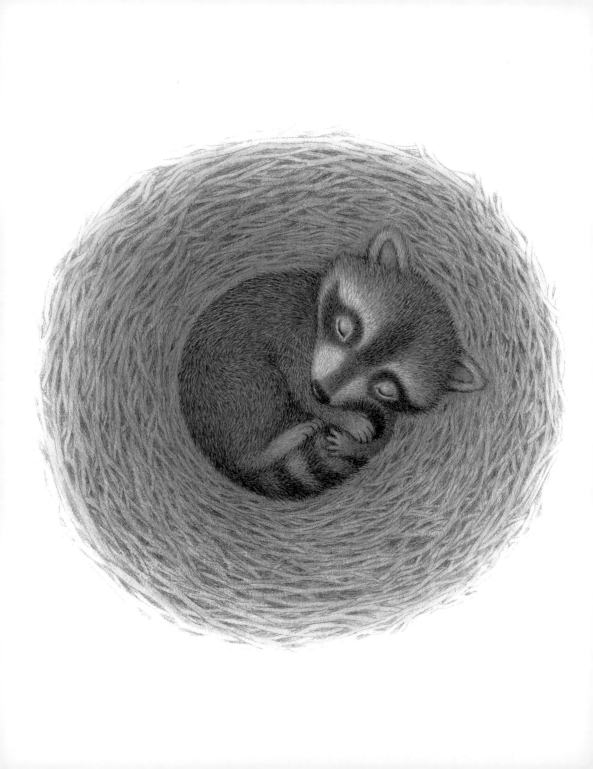

Pay attention to what touches your heart.
What is happening around you matters less than
what is happening within you.

Choose to believe in your own possibilities.
Love who you are, who you've been, and who you are becoming.
No one has seen tomorrow.

A dream is an open door to a brighter world.

Jump on through!

COMPENDIUM®
live inspired

Written by: Kobi Yamada
Illustrated by: Charles Santoso
Edited by: Amelia Riedler
Art Directed by: Justine Edge

Library of Congress Control Number: 2023934082 | ISBN: 978-1-957891-06-4

2nd printing. Printed in China with soy inks on FSC®-Mix certified paper.

Create meaningful moments with gifts that inspire.

CONNECT WITH US
live-inspired.com | sayhello@compendiuminc.com

 @compendiumliveinspired
#compendiumliveinspired